MODERN
RETRO
HOME

MODERN RETRO HOME

MR JASON GRANT

Photography by Lauren Bamford

hardie grant books

*This book is dedicated to my parents
and all my cheerleaders, who believe in me –
I'm lucky to be living my dream!*

TABLE OF CONTENTS

INTRODUCTION

What is modern retro? For me it's about being inspired by the iconic design decades and styles of the '50s, '60s, '70s and even the '80s – the architecture, furnishings, the colour palettes and decorative touches – and weaving those elements into a contemporary setting for today's lifestyle.

I've learnt a few things as a stylist: there are no hard and fast rules. Sometimes you might decide to overhaul your whole look or splurge on a new sofa with sleek modernist lines. Other times it might be a tiny edit ... move something here or there, add a shagpile rug, change a colour, include a stylish retro lamp.

Most of the people whose houses are included in this book work in creative fields – they are designers, stylists, gardeners and photographers. In their homes, they blend new and old, modern and retro, practical and personal. Their styling references elements of classic design eras, while also letting their personalities and lifestyles shine through. Each home is an individual take on what it might mean to furnish in a modern retro style.

I think it's fun to see how other people put together both the necessities and the treasures that they love. I hope you can open the book at any page and connect in some way. Perhaps you'll see something you can take away – an idea, a way of setting up a room or creating a wall of art or even just a colour combination. Most of all, I hope this book inspires you to create a home that expresses your own style.

LIVING

THE LIVING ROOM –
A CASUAL FEEL-GOOD SPACE

There's definitely been a shift since the 1950s to a much more casual lifestyle and more flexibility in how we live in our houses.

Innovative designers and architects from the 1930s onwards began to re-think how houses served people's needs. They started to create more open-plan living spaces inside, and opened houses up to the outside with walls of glass. By the 1950s and '60s, progressive design had filtered beyond architecture and became accessible to more people.

Designers began using new materials: chrome, plastics and fibreglass. They also experimented with new techniques, resulting in plywood and moulded forms. Innovative designs, especially in furniture and light fittings, were often well ahead of their time and were suited to mass production. Today, many of these pieces have become classics, their timeless modern looks perfectly at home in contemporary interior settings.

While open-plan rooms are now common, we're looking again at how they were handled in the '50s and '60s. Room dividers and open shelving are back in fashion, often used to create a separate zone without blocking light. Interesting pendant lights with retro profiles are replacing banks of ceiling lights. And greenery is again taking its place in our living spaces.

The fiddle leaf fig fills the corner and softens this room's look, linking the artist-owner's painting, the zigzag orange Jieldé lamp, spindle-back bench and elegant low-slung grey sofa. The bullet planter is an iconic retro shape – there are modern takes on this, though you may pick up an original online or at a garage sale.

Jason's Takeaway

Putting a plant in a raised pot gives it extra height and presence in the room.

This pink Panton chair seems as much like a sculpture as a place to sit. It's cleverly positioned next to an ethnic table, a perfect marriage of old and new.

Jason's Takeaway

Even a striking piece of furniture or an interesting object will look better if it's carefully positioned.

An original studded leather sofa –
a genuine vintage find – is paired
with a Parker-style coffee table
and cowhide rug. The 'painting'
is a piece of Marimekko fabric
stretched on a frame – a smart
example of DIY art. The owner's
1960s and '70s furniture fits with
the building's 1960s architecture,
but the grey paint on the walls
adds a more contemporary touch.

Jason's Takeaway

Art doesn't have to be expensive.

While the architecture is of the Victorian era, the furnishings have a modern look. The armchair references 1950s plank design chairs, and the solid-coloured, textured rug also has a '50s/'60s feel. The oversize mirror throws light into the room.

Jason's Takeaway

If you want a mirror to throw light, but not be too much of a feature itself, choose one without a frame or with bevel edging.

There's a serious dose of retro here with the '70s macramé and plenty of rugs and throws on the sofa. The classic print of an Asian girl is by the artist Tretchikoff, who was hugely popular in the 1950s and '60s and the lush plants bring a little – or maybe a lot! – of the outside in.

Jason's Takeaway

A plant hanging from the ceiling is a cool retro idea and saves space. Keep things orderly (see the neatly stacked magazines) – collections don't have to mean clutter.

This room has quite a Scandi vibe with its pale colours, sheepskin rug and polished slate floors. While the low-slung sofa looks as though it could be from the '70s, it's new. This is a big room with big pieces – I love the giant potted plant and oversize artwork.

Jason's Takeaway

Working with scale can really change a room. When in doubt, it's often best to go big. A few large-scale pieces can transform a room.

A sofa with a mid-century silhouette, indoor plants and treasures like the embroidered Indian folk art make for a stylish room. And then there's the swing, a piece designed by the owners.

Jason's Takeaway

I love the swing – as much fun for big kids as for little kids. If you prefer something more comfy, choose one of the hanging rattan seats that were popular in the '60s. Make sure that your ceiling can support the weight.

Furs, a giant comfy sofa, colourful cushions, a traditional rug, the timber-lined ceiling and the black feature wall make for a relaxed country retreat. The large paintings and big ceramic vase with tall branches suit the scale of the room while the bare floor-to-ceiling windows let the light flood in. The dramatic black wall is balanced by the dark sofa.

Jason's Takeway

Using two or three big areas of the same or a similar colour creates harmony in a room.

WALL
ART

- ▶ Hang multiple artworks to make a feature wall.

- ▶ Create impact by limiting the colour palette. Monochromatic with black and white is a design favourite, though you can also add pops of colour.

- ▶ Keep the framing the same – or similar – both in style or colour. You could choose a theme or a type of painting (oil painting, or graphic art). And hang works close together so they relate.

- ▶ A narrow space such as a hallway can work as a gallery wall for art or family photos.

If in doubt when hanging paintings, hang the artworks at eye level. Line up the tops and aim for a consistent distance between them.

Jason's Takeaway

Art doesn't have to be expensive. Seek out garage-sale and thrift-store finds that can add to the retro look, or swap artwork with friends.

WALL ART

- ▶ Wall art can be a collage of constantly changing artwork, messages, invitations and cards. Take the time to arrange your pieces and make sure you edit them into some order.

- ▶ Lean paintings against the wall or on a shelf (a perfect option if you are renting). This creates a different, more casual dynamic – and you can easily move pieces to freshen up the display.

WALL ART

An organic-shaped mobile, a minimalist painting and superb vintage wall light (almost a sculpture itself) create a quiet art moment (below).

Jason's Takeaway

You don't necessarily have to fill a wall – consider the negative spaces as part of the look.

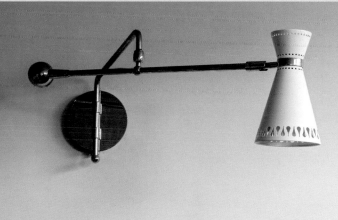

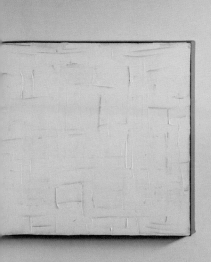

The woven string chair is modern but references '50s/'60s style. The fabulous aqua glass jar – a flea-market find – makes a colour-perfect vignette with the portrait. The trestle table with its cork top and the natural timber stools are well-priced High Street pieces.

Jason's Takeaway

Hunt down quirky or individual items that will add flair to basic flat-pack or budget furnishings.

This painting is powerful and busy and there's plenty of contrasting colour in the kilim rug, but the room doesn't feel hectic. It's quite considered. The original parachute-webbing chair and stool – signature designs from the '50s – draw your eye to the setting.

Jason's Takeaway

When you hang a painting, consider what's in front of and around it to get the best effect. And if you have a choice, always go for a big painting!

The bold colour of the carpet, a nostalgic nod to the colours of the '60s, makes a real impact.

Jason's Takeaway

If you don't want a colour to be too overwhelming, play it down. Here the vivid coral is offset by use of white and off-white with black and citrus green accents (another cool '60s shade).

An iconic leather lounge chair, timber and honey-coloured dining chairs and Berber-inspired rug have similar tones, and the rustic pottery echoes the autumnal shades, framed by the dark wall. The interplay of colours and textures defines this room.

Jason's Takeaway

Think texture as well as colour and tone. Polished timbers and sleek leather, embroidered textiles and nubbly shagpile rugs can all add character and depth.

The found object-cum-sculpture in the corner and the coffee table with its sturdy iron frame both say industrial, but the painting, tailored sofa and polished floors give the room a refined, urbane look. The contrasting styles sit comfortably together, softened by the shagpile rug.

Jason's Takeaway

You don't have to live in an industrial space or a loft to use objects or furniture with an industrial heritage.

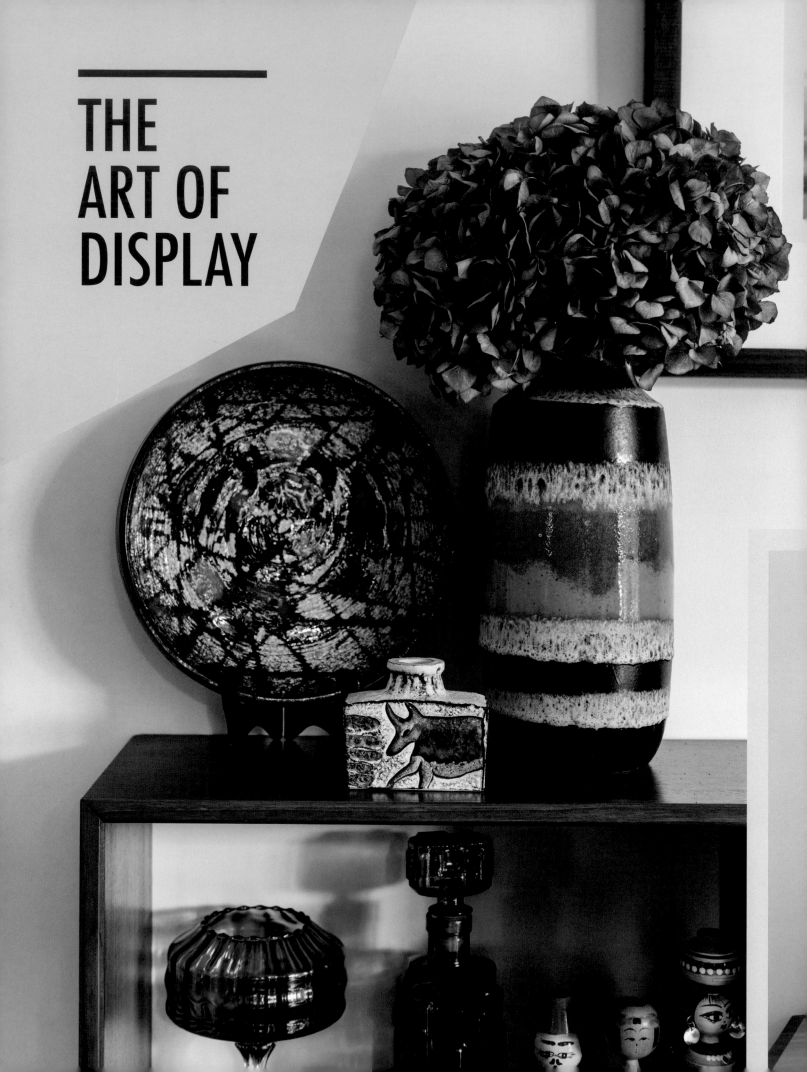

THE
ART OF
DISPLAY

A vignette can be a feel-good arrangement of favourite items, or a display of things you've collected. It's a decorating trick that can add a personal touch to your space.

▶ Give your display some height. You can work with a pyramid shape, putting smaller things at the side, taller in the centre.

▶ You can place objects in the same colour palette or tone together, then add one or two standout colours. Create a focal point.

▶ Add and subtract until you are happy with the final arrangement.

Edit! Editing and taking away pieces can be as important as what you add.

▶ You don't need to use everything you have in a display.

▶ While larger pieces of classic mid-century furniture may be too rare to find or too expensive to buy, it's still possible to pick up interesting smaller items such as pottery and ceramics. Put these collections on display to evoke those design eras.

▶ Flowers are great in any space, classic or contemporary.

THE ART OF
DISPLAY

THE ART OF
DISPLAY

Mix it up. Tribal with classic, neoclassical with Asian, polished with primitive. Sometimes controlled chaos makes for an amazing display. Forget the rules and just put pieces you love together. Place them close to artwork on the wall for an extra dimension. Retro pieces with a history or a story work especially well in these displays.

Framed vintage posters are a strong focus in this house. 'The multiple Le Corbusier drawings and posters hanging throughout reference the modernist roots and bones of the house', explains the owner.

Jason's Takeaway

Most of the artworks are framed in a timber similar in colour to the Scandinavian-design hide chairs and the robust shelving, creating unity.

The squishy Arfle Marenco sofa, which is new but a reissue of a '60s design, is piled with sheepskin, folk-art rugs and kilim cushions.

Jason's Takeaway

A sofa is an investment and sets the mood, the look and the tone of a space so it's an important starting point. Some of the key elements to consider are size (will it fit in the room); proportion (is the scale right for the room); and shape (tailored mid-century or laidback and casual). Comfort, colour and material are other critical considerations. Oh, and price.

Ethnic rugs and kilim-covered cushions on the sprawling sofa add a touch of '70s style and are a nod to the owner's frequent overseas travels.

Jason's Takeaway

Flat woven rugs known as kilims, traditionally from Turkey, Afghanistan and neighbouring regions, come in both bright patterns and (especially in older rugs) in more muted tones. They are versatile enough to suit everything from mid-century minimalism to a more eclectic boho look.

Dark-stained timber flooring
is the base for a classic Eames
armchair rocker. The bookshelves
behind have a story to tell, stacked
with more than just books.

Jason's Takeaway

**Leave some space on your
shelves to include photos
and objects that reflect your
interests and personal style.**

This living space flows from an open kitchen with breakfast bar to a casual dining setting and then on to the sofa and coffee table for relaxing. It's open plan, but each area has a different purpose and is defined by a different floor surface – from lino to slate to carpet.

Jason's Takeaway

Changing floor surfaces, or using rugs, will divide a space into zones or mini rooms without breaking up the flow.

This beautifully crafted sideboard adheres to the mid-century mantra of form follows function. It provides a balance to the large artworks hanging over it, and to the one stunning piece of pottery.

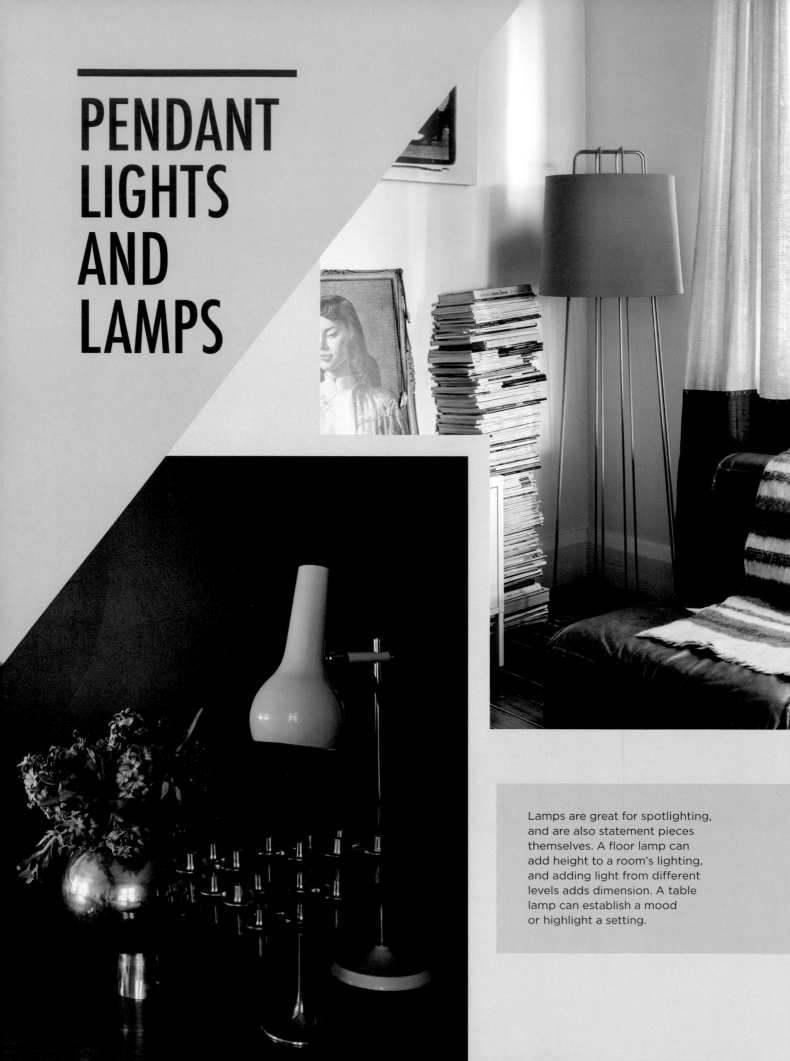

PENDANT
LIGHTS
AND
LAMPS

Lamps are great for spotlighting, and are also statement pieces themselves. A floor lamp can add height to a room's lighting, and adding light from different levels adds dimension. A table lamp can establish a mood or highlight a setting.

Pendants are functional but also highly decorative (in particular some of the inventive designs from the '50s and '60s), adding shape, scale and a distinctive look. They can cast an ambient light and create a focal point in a room.

Pendant lights can create a focus in a room by day as well as by night. You may be lucky enough to track down an original, such as the white vintage 1955 light by Finnish architect Alvar Aalto (far right), but a quirky chandelier-style beaded pendant or a minimal Chinese paper shade might suit your scheme just as well.

Jason's Takeaway

Take the time to choose a light fitting that adds to a room's personality and isn't an afterthought.

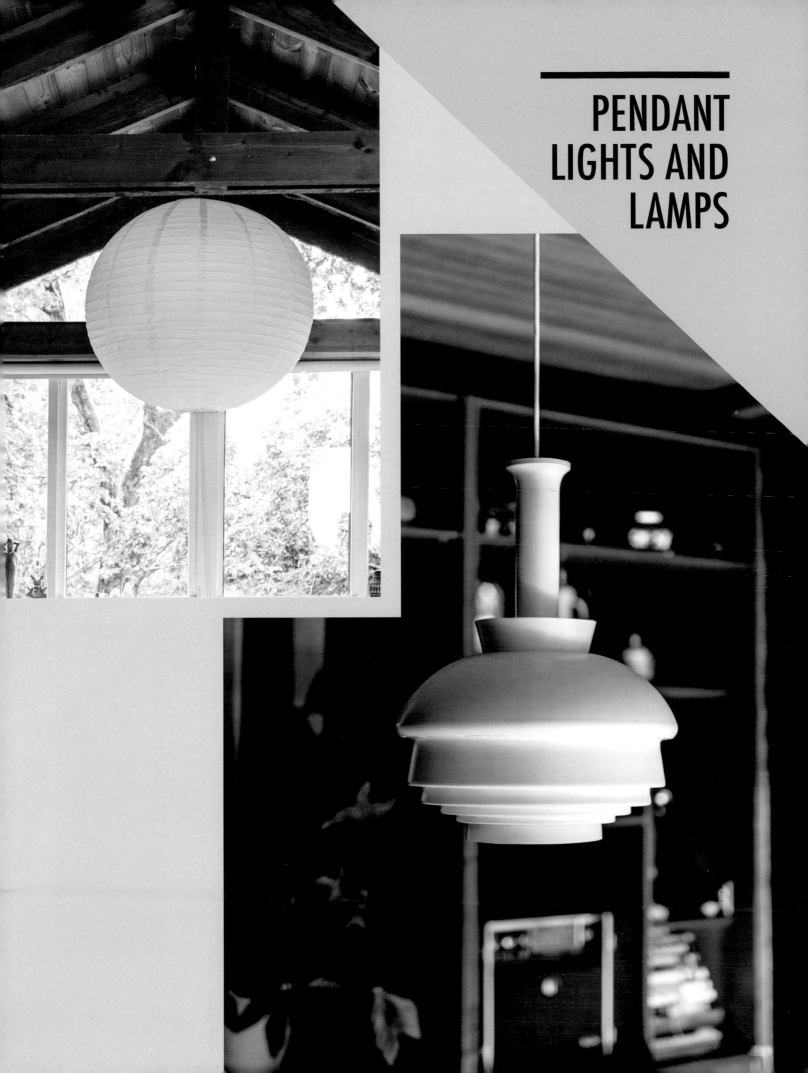

PENDANT LIGHTS AND LAMPS

The elegant round table and curving sofa pay homage to the organic shapes and attention to craftsmanship and detail favoured by mid-century designers.

Jason's Takeaway

Use contemporary furniture that celebrates another era for a 'new' modern retro look.

This is a very masculine – and maximalist – space. The owners have the confidence to mix genres and styles in their own, unique way. Thrift-shop chic meets vintage finds, classic pieces join favourite treasures and things have a patina of age. The room is shot through with blues and greys and interesting textures. It looks comfortable and lived in and the owners say it is 'continually evolving'.

Jason's Takeaway

Everything doesn't have to be perfect and it doesn't have to happen all at once. Search out pieces you love over time and that work for your lifestyle.

This is an Edwardian-era house with a simple modern twist. Cream, white and a palette of greys – the deep grey sofa, bluish-grey rug, dark timber floors and pumpkin-shaped dark grey knitted ottoman – sit comfortably in this light-filled room.

Jason's Takeaway

You don't have to go with the era of a house. One option is to paint your room in a neutral tone to create a canvas for any style you like. And remember that dark colours can be neutrals too.

This curated corner features a preloved red metal table, pencil and wash drawings and red and yellow glazed ceramics. The sofa is modern, an English/Americana classic with little turned legs, covered in a subtle grey linen. As the owner explains, 'We like things from every era; it's a Victorian house but we have many classic and retro pieces.'

The tan leather sofa creates an interesting contrast with the grey concrete wall and painting.

Jason's Takeaway

A considered mix of textures and colours livens up any space.

SOFT
FURNISHINGS

Layering rugs, pillows and throws adds depth, colour and texture to a room. For rugs, try overlapping a solid colour with a pattern.

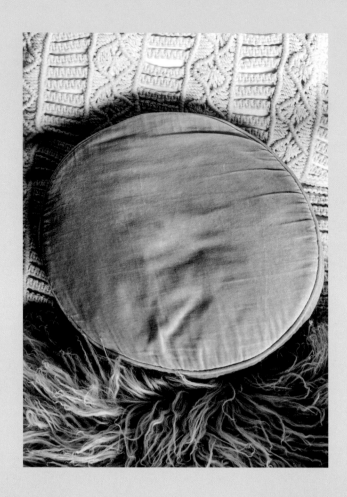

SOFT FURNISHINGS

When it comes to cushions, for some people it's the more the merrier. They certainly up the comfort level.

▸ Try mixing solids with patterns, different textures and different size cushions. Or stick to one colour – rules are made to be broken!

▸ If you want to mix patterns, look for a common colour. The black in the floral and in the graphic on the cushions (below) lets the clashing patterns work together.

There's more than a little nostalgia in some soft furnishings. Floor rugs, pillows and throws can conjure up different eras and design styles – flokati rugs recall the '60s, woven and knitted textiles and velvet cushions introduce a '70s vibe and furs have a Scandi look.

SOFT
FURNISHINGS

A built-in banquette (with storage space below an added bonus) makes the ideal nook for reading or relaxing.

Jason's Takeaway

You don't need a big space to create a retreat.

This room is pure Hollywood. Or maybe it's Palm Springs? The luxurious white leather sofas and two-tone purple rug, which looks like a piece of '60s op art, definitely make a design statement.

Jason's Takeaway

Balance a bold solid colour with a bold pattern so one doesn't outshine the other.

With the Danish-design wing chair,
blonde wood, fur throws, vintage
suitcase and an amazing brick
fireplace to the ceiling there's a
mountain-lodge flavour to this room.
A focal point is the original 1960s
C. Jere metal sculpture above the
fireplace. The owners bought it on
eBay for collection in the US when
they were visiting. 'We got it home
(eventually!) and I love the fact that
it takes pride of place at our home.'

Jason's Takeaway

**The pale cream and white
furnishings leave the focus on
the fireplace and sculpture.**

There's a little bit of everything here – iconic silver '60s Arco-style lamp, psychedelic wall art, flower-patterned sofa scattered with graphic black and white cushions and a futurist table on spiky orange legs. At the same time it's quite controlled and balanced.

Jason's Takeaway

The black in the flower-patterned sofa and the black leather sofa really ground this look.

The pea-green Eames moulded plywood chair provides a shot of colour against the dark floorboards and rug and bright white walls.

Jason's Takeaway

A chair such as this, the original design dating from 1946, instantly says mid-century modern. You don't need a set of them – just one will evoke that design-savvy time and add serious style to any interior, modern or retro.

ON THE SHELF

In the '50s and '60s, as rooms became more open plan, room dividers became a way of defining different spaces while still letting you see through to the next room. Shelving units, like large paintings and wall hangings, can give height to a room, carrying the eye up. Remember not to fill the shelves to overflowing but leave a little space. A plant, especially a cascading one, can soften the look.

Recessed shelves combine a smart architectural idea (using a wall cavity) with something designers (and you) will love – a place to arrange favourite objects, books, travel souvenirs and more. Arrange things on the shelves as if you are telling a story. Colour-block books to create a pattern, include unusual objects (but not too many at once) and add a vase or photos.

ON THE
SHELF

Cushions are an easy, affordable way to update a room. And you can change them with the seasons. Here, yellow, blue and white add a nautical, summery note to this fine-lined minimalist sofa, while opposite, the patterned cushion adds a pop of colour to the grey fabric of the sofa. In winter you might use velvet cushions or a fur throw.

This chic beach shack blurs the lines between old and new. The angled lamp, shagpile carpet and kilim-covered cushions say modernist, but in a casual way. Special pieces include a vintage tribal mirror from etsy France and two linen swing chairs. The showstopper is the stained black timber wall (using stain instead of paint lets some of the grain show through).

Jason's Takeaway

A beach house doesn't have to be blue and white, as this shack proves.

While many of the original elements of this 1970s mountain cottage have been retained, such as the wood-panelled walls, the main features are the owner's period pieces: a teak sideboard, old-time radio, record player, pottery lamp, and hanging ukulele and banjo. The round shadowbox, filled with the owner's mementos, adds to the relaxed holiday vibe.

Jason's Takeaway

Home is where the heart is, so collect and display pieces you love.

White walls and white floors in this art deco apartment create a cocoon for the stylist-owner's signature collection of casual sofas, old-world artworks, vases and collectables. Lynda is a master at creating a calm, relaxed vibe.

Jason's Takeaway

Try some of Lynda's tricks to introduce a casual look, such as the unstructured sofa in crushed linen with mismatched cushions. The unframed artwork is just pinned on the wall, and the rustic table and textured grey planter are easy-going accessories.

A Scotty dog lamp and old-fashioned toys, such as a top, sit on a well-worn travelling trunk. The boucherouite rug is a traditional Moroccan rag rug, crafted from offcuts of fabric, that adds texture and picks up the colours of the timber walls and doors.

Jason's Takeaway

A rug with this much character is really like an artwork. Using an unusual or colourful rug can lift the whole room.

Plants with giant leaves, glossy earthenware pots and a bright yellow stool matching the door make for a welcoming entrance.

Jason's Takeaway

If you have large windows to screen, place pots on stools or into raised planters to make a natural screen that also filters the light.

The artist-owner's personality is reflected in the mishmash of colour and creativity – patchwork quilt, velvet cushions, kilim floor rug, Mexican knick-knacks, cactus plants, chalkboard wall, and a fun collection dangling from an iconic Eames-style 'hang-it-all' rack. Pink is a consistent colour note though – in the rug, the wall, the paintings and other items.

Jason's Takeaway

Colour is one of the key ways to tie a look together.

GOING GREEN

Indoor plants are definitely having a moment. Again. In the '50s and '60s plants became an essential part of interiors. Architecture and furniture focused on organic and geometric shapes, and cactus and dramatic plants, such as Philodendron, were chosen to echo these forms. By the 1970s, the more greenery the better, with rubber plants, figs, ferns and spider plants flourishing indoors. Now plants are a must-have in interiors all over again.

Plants add a feeling of calm and freshness and soften a space. As well as water, they need light, so pop them next to a window to keep them growing and healthy.

GOING GREEN

A Noguchi-style paper lamp, the soft green shades of a botanical painting and leafy potplants give this corner an almost Japanese aesthetic.

Jason's Takeaway

Position potplants in relation to lamps, furniture or artwork, so you can tell a story or create a particular effect.

GOING GREEN

GOING
GREEN

Jason's Takeaway

Planters can help set the retro mood you're after. Bullet-shaped planters are a slick choice for mid-century flair, handmade pottery and ceramic pots are typically '60s and '70s, while macramé hanging baskets make for a cool hippy style. Cluster small pots together.

GOING
GREEN

Jason's Takeaway

You can use striking plant pots as focal points in your styling – their texture and colour will add personality to your rooms. Look for quirky designs, retro shades and interesting patterns and materials. Woven basket pots have a great '60s and '70s vibe.

STUDY

We all need a little space where we can check our mail or catch up on some reading or even have a mini home office. It's not always possible to have a spare room, but it is possible to carve out a corner or nook and make it your own. Quirky additions, such as old ballot boxes or a terrarium, add a personal note.

Double windows plus white walls and white blinds mean this room is flooded with light. A designer chair and slim built-in desk, primitive artefacts and fresh flowers keep it natural.

Jason's Takeaway

A cantilevered desk gives an illusion of space, leaving the area below uncluttered. It also makes it easier to slip a chair in when it's not being used.

A Parker-style desk, a Casala designer chair – a favourite from the 1970s with its innovative swooping shape – distinctive artwork and greenery are tucked effectively into a compact space.

Jason's Takeaway

This is part of a larger room but it works as a self-contained study or work corner because it's well planned. I love that chair!

TOM FORD

STUDY

HALLWAYS
AND
STAIRWAYS

Jason's Takeaway

Hallways and stairways are sometimes ignored, left blank and awkward – a lost opportunity to offer a welcome to visitors and establish your style throughout the house. Add your touch to these spaces with rugs, artwork, plants and strategically placed pieces of furniture.

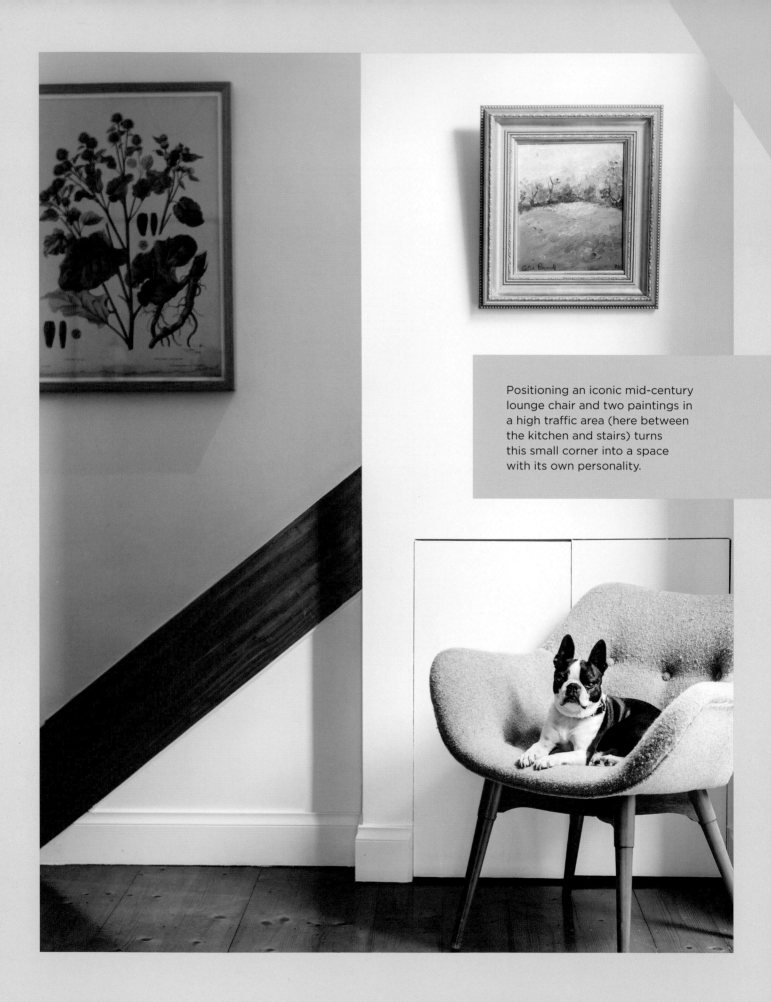

Positioning an iconic mid-century lounge chair and two paintings in a high traffic area (here between the kitchen and stairs) turns this small corner into a space with its own personality.

HALLWAYS AND STAIRWAYS

More than just a stairway – almost a room in itself – this space includes artwork, shelves loaded with eclectic treasures from the owners' travels, as well as books and greenery.

A bright, textured rag rug and a richly embroidered and tasselled textile over the door in this hall capture the spirit of playful, retro and bohemian that fill this artist's house.

Jason's Takeaway

If there's a theme or mood in the house, continue it in the hall.

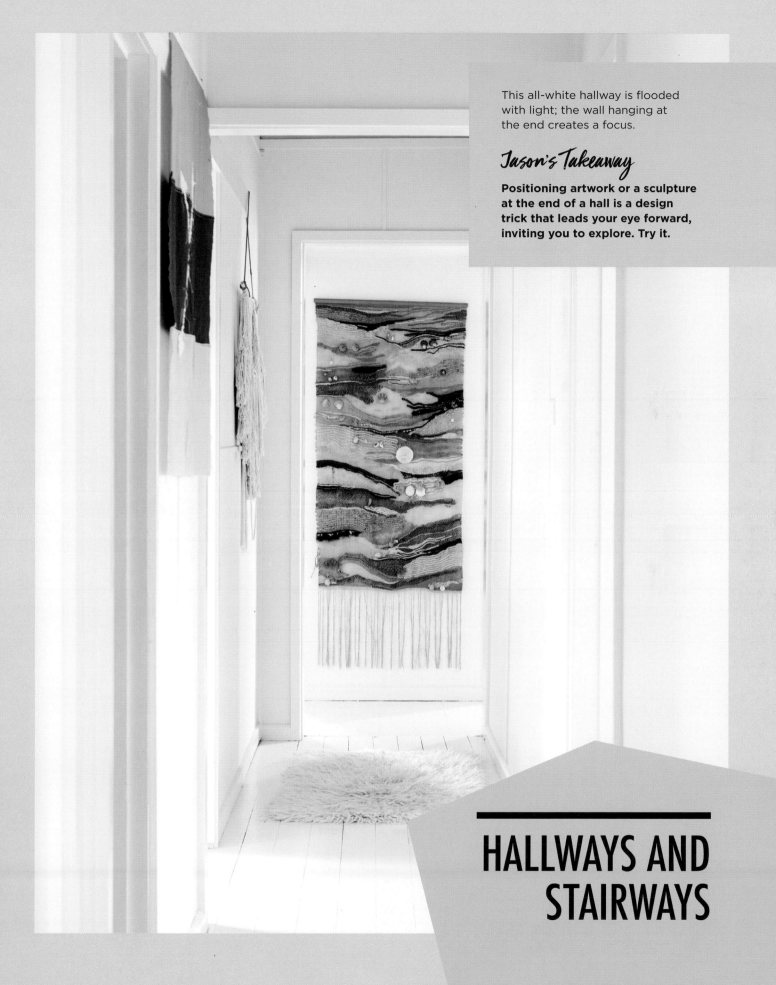

This all-white hallway is flooded with light; the wall hanging at the end creates a focus.

Jason's Takeaway

Positioning artwork or a sculpture at the end of a hall is a design trick that leads your eye forward, inviting you to explore. Try it.

HALLWAYS AND STAIRWAYS

Woven raffia Balinese runners on dark floors, sculptural wall art and a shapely Tom Dixon pendant lamp add interest to a long narrow hall.

HALLWAYS AND STAIRWAYS

An oversized painting and stools with woven seats add warmth and personality to this hallway.

Jason's Takeaway

A single large painting can create impact on an otherwise white wall. Choose colours based on the mood you want to create.

HANG
IT UP

Colourful shopping bags become
virtual artworks when hung on a
wall. A ribbon-like sculptural hook
holds a French market basket and
old-fashioned skipping rope and
vintage timber spools become
hooks for hallway necessities.

Jason's Takeaway

**Use hangers or retro hooks to
imbue character to almost any
wall space, hall space or corner.
Think function *and* fun.**

KITCHEN

THE KITCHEN –
A NEW MEETING PLACE

Kitchens are increasingly the hub of the house, a casual meeting place for family and friends who like to be where the action is. Equipment may be high tech (induction stoves, microwaves, espresso machines), but retro elements can introduce contrast and character.

In the '50s and '60s, kitchens began to open up to the rest of the house, featuring a large servery or breakfast bar. Sometimes they would completely open up to a living space, patio or even have a garden view.

These days, an open kitchen is standard and a bar is almost essential, frequently used for breakfast, lunch and even dinner. A favourite retro addition is to use stools with a vintage pedigree. They might be original, re-editions or replicas – their versatile designs allow for a personal touch and suit many different kitchen looks.

Pendant lights over the bar are practical and can also echo quirky, elegant or retro industrial styles. Bold wallpaper offers another option for a blast from the past. Adding greenery is a way to bring the outside in and to soften the look of a kitchen's hard surfaces.

FlowerPot pendant lights by Danish designer Verner Panton are a classic '60s shape, but they look contemporary, and so does the Atomica coffee pot, another iconic piece. Just outside the kitchen is a vintage Grant Featherstone design chair.

Jason's Takeaway

Choosing iconic shapes and classic designs, either genuine vintage finds, replicas, or even modern pieces inspired by the originals, is a way of introducing a retro element and changing the whole dynamic.

FOR LIKE EVER

A mix of closed and open shelving provides a venue for the owner's curated kitchenware.

Jason's Takeaway

A place for everything and everything in its place. Even utilitarian things can make a display if grouped by colour or size or shape.

There's a serene, calm look to this all-white kitchen. The glossy and matt surfaces, vertical panels on the cupboards and horizontal detail on the gauzy blinds take the style up a notch or two.

Jason's Takeaway

If you choose to use one colour, layer it with different tones, surface finishes and textures.

This kitchen is something of a gallery space, with its neon art (made by the owner), pop art pink stool, masks, bleached skull, icons and eye-catching painting all carefully curated.

Jason's Takeaway

Artworks can define your unique style in any room of the house – even in the kitchen.

IT'S
IN THE
DETAILS

In the kitchen both day-to-day necessities as well as beautiful objects can be arranged to make a personal display. Small trays keep kitchen essentials (salt, pepper, napkins) neat but looking good, and where space is limited it also means things can easily be moved.

IT'S IN THE
DETAILS

Open shelving is an invitation to add personality to a room. These asymmetric shelves are in a bright modern kitchen, but the carefully composed objects range from classical sculpture to a lovely art deco teapot, turned timber fruit and a Fornasetti plate.

Jason's Takeaway

The trick with such displays is to keep moving pieces until you are satisfied with the arrangement. It takes a little practice but the results are worth it.

Jason's Takeaway

Sometimes the kitchen is underrated as a place where you can show your style but I think any space can be used.

IT'S IN THE
DETAILS

Time-worn timber chopping boards, fresh fruit, finely turned Japanese-style boxes and bowls and even retro flower-printed Pyrex casserole dishes all make for interesting displays when creatively arranged.

IT'S IN THE DETAILS

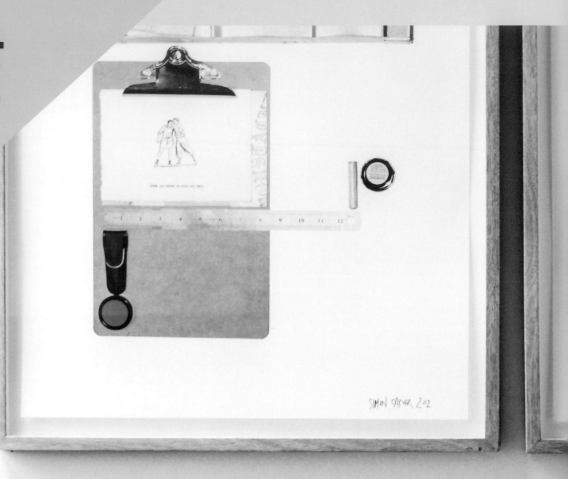

A toaster, kettle and old-time willow pattern teacups become a still life setting when neatly arranged on a yellow tray next to a vintage timber box.

IT'S IN THE DETAILS

Natural materials such as pottery and timber have their own inherent good looks. Bring a stylist's eye to your kitchen by colour-blocking your mugs, grouping kitchen boards or piling fruit into an old-school wire basket.

In a fantastic old apartment block 'filled with collections both old and new, found and bought', as the stylist–owner says, this kitchen blends perfect with imperfect. The monochrome colours extend from the black, grey and white tiled floor to the stripped-back walls and the silvery wire mesh of the light fitting.

Jason's Takeaway

When working with a monochrome colour scheme pay attention to patterns and shapes, different surfaces and textures for maximum effect.

Natural timber adds a little colour to this grey and white kitchen setting.

This kitchen has a relaxed farmhouse feel. Recycled cupboards sit on the mantle, there's a work-friendly bench that does double duty as storage, and paired industrial pendant lights add character to the room.

Jason's Takeaway

Things in this kitchen are sturdy and generous in size so choosing a pair of bold industrial light fittings on chains matches the scale.

A graphic hand-painted mural adds personality to this kitchen in an inner-city terrace house.

Jason's Takeaway

Art can have a place in any room, including the kitchen.

The kitchen on the opposite page looks futuristic, in a 1960s *Barbarella* way, with its sharp sci-fi angles and sophisticated combination of black timber, marble, concrete and metal. The kitchen below has an '80s luxe style with bronze and marble.

Jason's Takeaway

Both kitchens are small, but the reflective bronze metal finish on surfaces reflects light and creates the illusion of more space.

This modern pendant light is a whimsical take on a chandelier.

Jason's Takeaway

The chandelier is a statement piece but because it's white – the same colour as the walls and fittings – it doesn't overwhelm the room. And I think it's fun.

Storage spaces can be style statements in their own right – the bright yellow wall cupboard is the focal point of this kitchen space. The big white door handles reference the benchtops and create a sense of unity in the design.

A few little bursts of retro orange and bright yellow contrast with the black tapware and lamp.

Jason's Takeaway

Add a lamp in the kitchen for task lighting or to spotlight a favourite object. It's also ideal if you want more lighting without altering the existing fittings.

Black and white is timeless, but adding a fabulous yellow planter and three lovely flowery vintage tiles gives this kitchen an instant lift.

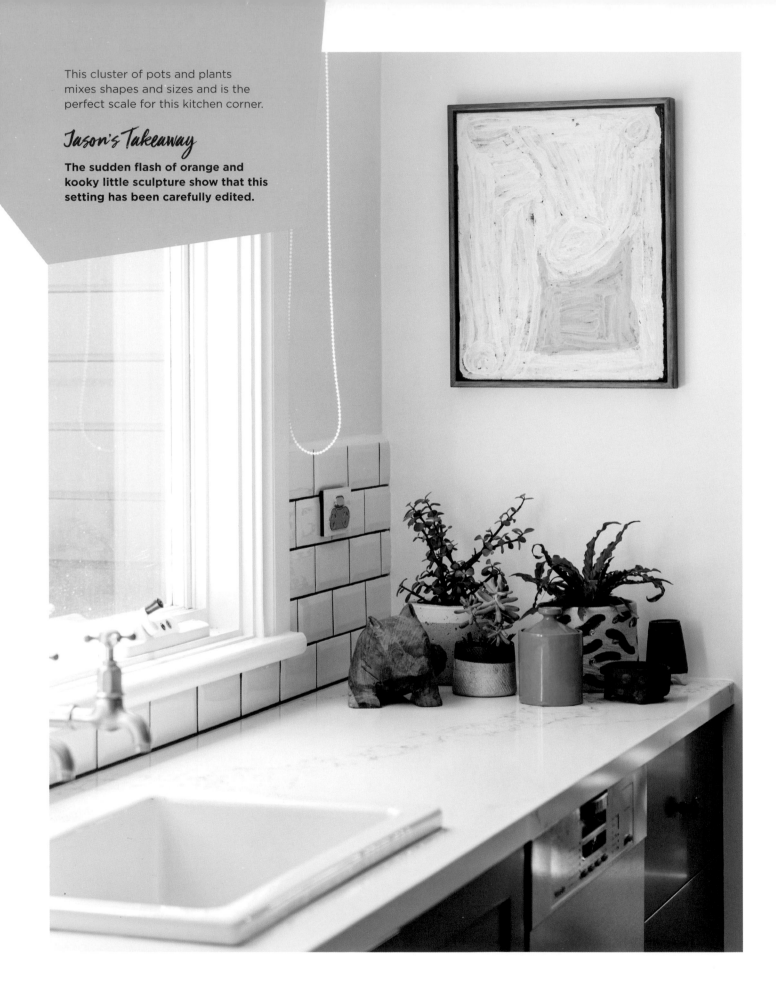

This cluster of pots and plants mixes shapes and sizes and is the perfect scale for this kitchen corner.

Jason's Takeaway

The sudden flash of orange and kooky little sculpture show that this setting has been carefully edited.

A palette of silvery greys and kitchen implements displayed as much for their good looks as their practicality give character to this kitchen space.

The flower-power splashback, sleek timber cupboards and patterned ceramic canisters definitely say Brady Bunch.

Jason's Takeaway

Boldly patterned and coloured wallpapers are an easy and cost-effective way to add a retro '60s or '70s tone to your kitchen. If you don't want it to be *too* funky, keep the wallpaper to one wall and don't add other patterns.

The underlying style of this home is '70s nostalgia, an era the owners love. Greenery, from the fern on the fridge to the fresh greens in a jar, adds to the laid-back look.

Jason's Takeaway

Indoor plants are great, but even a generous bunch of herbs can make a display. Work with what you have.

There's a friendly, makeshift quality to this kitchen with its crowded shelves, old-fashioned canisters, pots and ceramics. I like the idea of a blackboard wall – it's fun and practical, because you can draw, doodle or just write your shopping list.

Jason's Takeaway

You can apply the blackboard paint like any wall paint.

AT THE
BAR

In the '50s and '60s, as kitchens became more sociable and eating more casual, 'kitchen bars' became fashionable. These days a bar and stools are almost essential in any kitchen. French-style café stools and lattice rattan stools with a casual Tiki Bar style are just two of the stool styles that can introduce a retro vibe.

Sharply angular vintage designer stools and the yellow Tolix-style stools (opposite), a classic French-design that first appeared in the 1940s, show how different designs can set the tone for your kitchen.

AT THE BAR

Jason's Takeaway

Make sure to measure the height of your bar before choosing your stools. Other things to consider are if you want a back or not; arms or not; upholstery or not; and the material (metal, timber, rattan). Are the stools adjustable for people of different heights? Size is important, too. How many can you fit at the bar – and will stools tuck under it if necessary?

DINING

THE DINING AREA – MORE THAN A ROOM FOR MEALS

Since the 1950s and '60s, dining, living and kitchen areas have become increasingly integrated, often forming one large, open space – the separate dining room has all but disappeared. Today's dining 'room' is a casual and relaxed place for eating, but also likely does double or triple duty as work area, meeting place and planning centre.

One area of mid-century design mastery was chair design, and the creative shapes from that era include some outstanding dining chairs. The range of styles is wide, from the works of unknown designers to the cult classics: the crafted timbers of Danish modern, the refined Hans Wegner Wishbone chair, Ray and Charles Eames' moulded-plastic chairs with their splayed Eiffel Tower legs or the curvy, space-age forms of Italian Casala chairs.

Even within a living space, you can create a dining area that channels the retro design aesthetic and sits comfortably within the most modern interior scheme.

Reflective bronze-metal cupboards mix with old-fashioned spindle-back chairs and an industrial pendant. Grandma-esque cushions, ethnic throws and floor rugs add more layers. You can glimpse the Smeg fridge – modern but iconic and retro in shape. The look is eclectic, but it's softened by the colours (silvers, gold, pinks, soft blues) and the greenery.

Jason's Takeaway

You don't have to use pieces all from one period or style to furnish a room, but look for colours that pull it together.

The furniture is from different eras (the Eiffel chairs are mid-century classics) but the warm timber colours and bright patterns of the kilim link the different elements.

Jason's Takeaway

Placing a dining table on a rug helps create a dining 'zone' within a larger open-plan room.

Danish-design mid-century
Wishbone chairs, a distressed
vintage timber table – originally
an old packing table – one
perfectly simple green bowl and
an eye-catching painting give
this room a unique personality.

Jason's Takeaway

**This room is minimally furnished but
an intriguing mix of old and new.**

This calm space is light in colour but rich with texture, from the subtly different timbers and white gloss table to the plaid rugs, leafy greenery and ceramics.

Jason's Takeaway

If you're working with all white, or a neutral palette of blonde, beige and white, create focus by introducing varied textures.

The setting here is all about low-key luxury. The tribal Ikat fabric on the chairs is an exotic note. The pendant lightshade is oversized and unexpected, contrasting a business-like grey flannel with glossy gold lining.

Jason's Takeaway

A pendant lamp is perfect for a dining setting, especially if the light shines down to focus on the table.

This room seems a perfect time capsule, a chic Palm Springs–style breakfast room from another era, with rattan and smoked glass table, vintage rattan and iron chairs with tropical cushions, and jute rug.

Geometric artwork, a stack of colour-blocked cushions and the sculptural grid of Bertoia-style chairs stand out against the dark wall.

Jason's Takeaway

A dark feature wall highlights art and furniture. It can be used to define a separate zone (here it separates the kitchen from the dining space) in an open-plan area.

A Tolomeo mega floor lamp, timber table, Bertoia dining chair, a chrome and leather Eames style chair and in the background, an orange–red lacquered Chinese wedding cabinet and leather and fabric ottomans – there's a lot going on, but no one element dominates. Blue and orange accents and the many textures create a subtle harmony.

There's a minimalist feeling to this setting with the focus on the modernist artwork, an original print the owners bought in Europe. Thonet Bentwood chairs surround a simple trestle table and an articulated industrial Jieldé lamp contrasts with a sweet little pendant lamp with a delicate frill.

Jason's Takeaway

These two lights, both retro, couldn't be more different. They set a mood at night by providing different light sources, and their contrasting profiles look great in the day as well.

I love this fiddle leaf fig – king of the retro plant world – sitting in a brown paper shopping bag, an ingenious and budget way to hide an ugly pot. The white Casalino chairs, a 1970s design, paired with an iconic tulip table suit the compact space.

Jason's Takeaway

Round tables are a great solution if space is tight. They take up less room (less sharp angles to bump into) and if they have a central leg, there's more room under them as well (both for your legs and chair legs).

Fabulous tangerine-coloured Italian designer chairs contrast with a cork-top table from a collection that English designer Ilse Crawford did in collaboration with Ikea.

Jason's Takeaway

Genuine designer pieces can be an expensive investment, but if paired with budget buys you can introduce an individual look without breaking the bank.

The owners of this house have a casual and earthy quality that's conveyed in their space. The chairs are vintage but the table is new. An ethnic rug, rustic stools, an ottoman and large planters are all linked by the warm brown, russet and orange colours.

The charm of this small dining space is its mismatched seating arrangement. Each chair – and the stool – has its own, unique character.

Jason's Takeaway

Not everything has to match, but a common element can make disparate things work together. These chairs are all quite fine, and all have similar dark colours.

An Arco Italian design floor lamp, blonde wood table and spiky vintage dining chairs on bright coral carpet make for a perfect time capsule of a room. Original orange and yellow pottery adds the finishing touch.

Jason's Takeaway

Add a dash of period flair by including small objects such as original ceramic vases and pots. Hunt them down in markets, garage sales, vintage or thrift shops.

This is a very urban space. It could be a Brooklyn loft, or somewhere in Europe. Exposing part of the existing brick wall and leaving sketches made on the walls during construction are a clue to the building's heritage as a worker's cottage. The chair references the postmodern Memphis style of the '80s.

Jason's Takeaway

It's not about having lots of pieces – an interesting idea or unusual object can add a wow factor.

Many of the chair designs of the '40s and '50s in particular were unexpected, even startling, but today their iconic silhouettes sit comfortably in almost any interior style. These Eames-style chairs are a cult classic.

Mid-century-inspired chairs and a stylish table that is new but timeless in design, plus vivid colours (especially that pink sideboard) make for a pared-back but powerful look. The pendant light is a Scandinavian design, a modern take on an industrial shape, but made from soft silicon rubber in a brilliant yellow.

Jason's Takeaway

Be brave. If you love colour, use it.

BEDROOM

THE BEDROOM – YOUR PERSONAL SANCTUARY

In many ways, bedrooms have not changed as much as other rooms in the house. I think a bedroom should be a sanctuary, a retreat where you can express your design style even more freely.

The bed almost inevitably dominates the room, and everything has to work around it. Colour-wise you might opt for soothing colours – either cool, pale shades or moody dark colours. A mid-century designer chair makes a striking feature (and is a comfy place to sit), even in an ultra-modern room. Unusual bedside lamps or a vintage pendant are easy ways to add character and a nod to another era.

If you are channelling a '70s vibe, you could layer some embroidered textiles and rugs. And if it's Danish design or a Scandi look you are after, you might consider going almost all white, with blonde timber furniture and soft furs. The bedroom is also where you can include a personal art collection or, if space allows, some vintage pottery, glassware or sculpture – the bedroom is where you can make your design dreams come true.

In a traditional terrace room with French doors opening onto a balcony, bedding adds a flash of up-to-the-minute colour.

I love the freshness of this room. It's modern with its big black-and-white photo and crisp white walls, but then there's that rustic tree-stump table, and floral and print pillowcases that strike a nostalgic note.

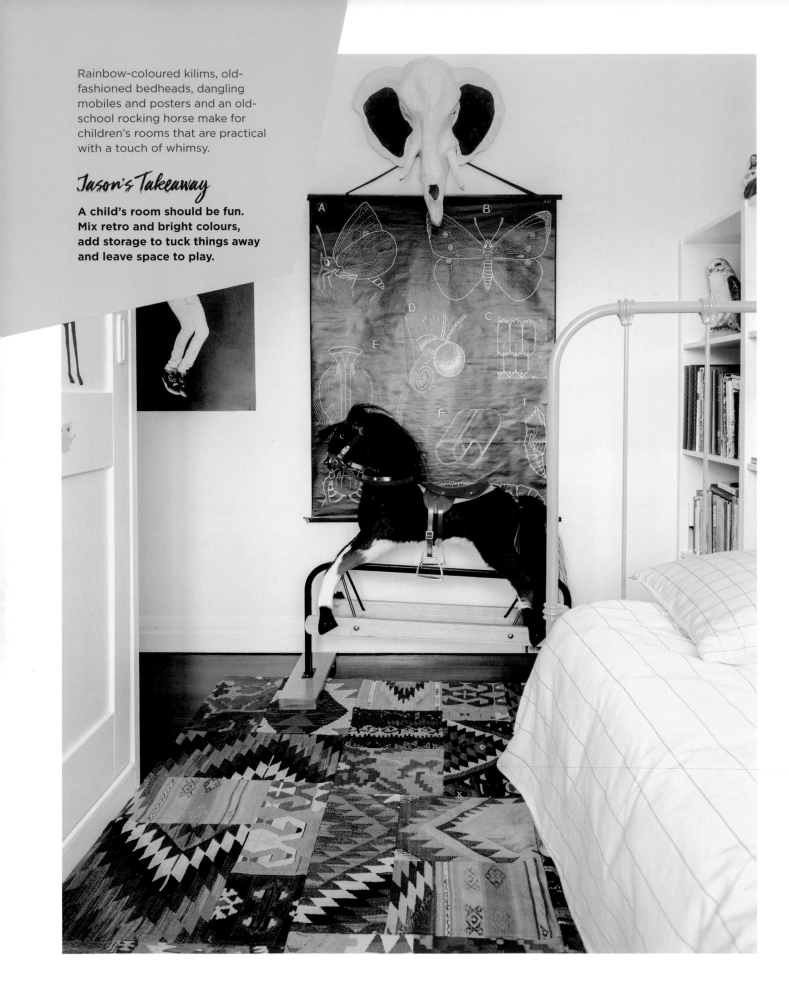

Rainbow-coloured kilims, old-fashioned bedheads, dangling mobiles and posters and an old-school rocking horse make for children's rooms that are practical with a touch of whimsy.

Jason's Takeaway

A child's room should be fun. Mix retro and bright colours, add storage to tuck things away and leave space to play.

A dark, moody wall, a mix of patterned pillowcases, and a cross-check bedcover channel a casual, relaxed feeling for this bedroom.

Jason's Takeaway

The dark colour for the wall is an unusual bedroom choice but it works because it's quite a soothing colour.

The exposed light bulb – looped and hanging at the side of the bed – frees up space on the bedside table. Plants and an oversized painting add personality and character.

This apartment is tiny, so a fold-down bed is just one of the ingenious solutions to make it work. Everything is very considered – the squishy tan leather sofa, polished floor, and moody dark surfaces. It has a masculine sensibility and a sophisticated edge.

Jason's Takeaway

A small space does not have to be white. Think outside the box with colours and finishes.

An unusual porthole window lets
light flood into this bedroom,
and pillows are piled high
for maximum comfort.

In this all-white, panelled room with its white curtains and white lights, the graphic quilt of grey and white with a narrow pink rim of colour stands out.

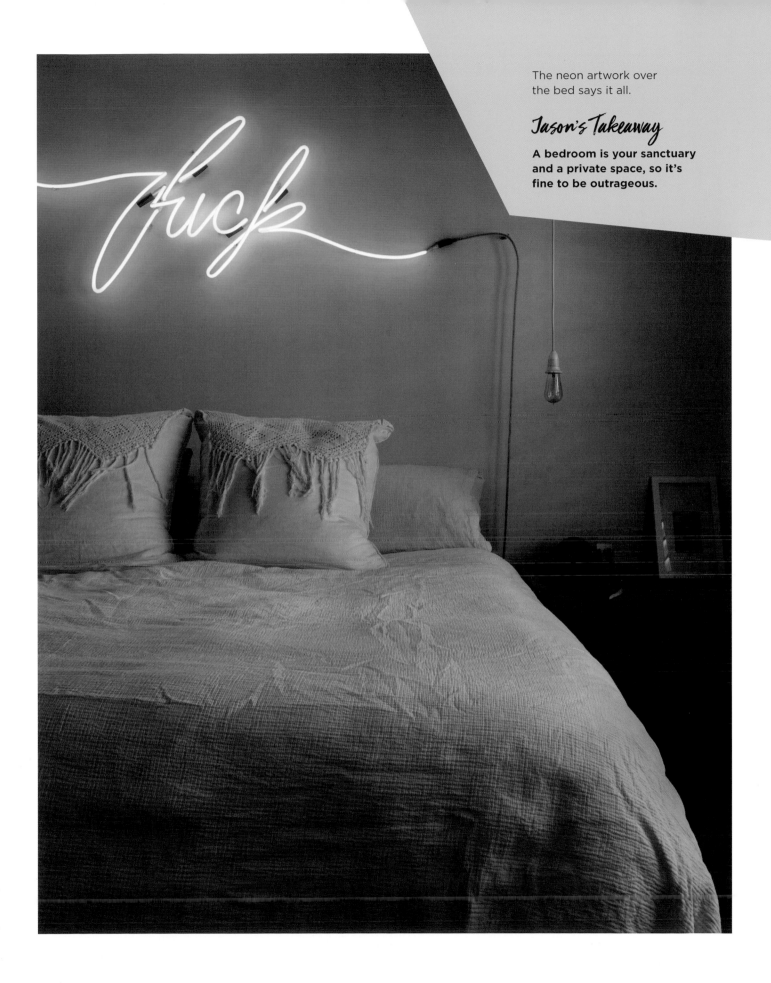

The neon artwork over the bed says it all.

Jason's Takeaway

A bedroom is your sanctuary and a private space, so it's fine to be outrageous.

BESIDE
THE
BED

Lamps are an easy way to introduce
a retro element. It's still possible
to source original lamps from the
'50s, '60s and '70s, and there are
replicas as well as shapes inspired
by modernist design. A vintage
metal anglepoise lamp with its
iconic '60s silhouette in the original
coffee colour and contemporary
timber-based lamps are just options.

Jason's Takeaway

**A bedside lamp can throw soft,
ambient light, just right for
a bedroom, but also focuses
light for bedtime reading.**

Jason's Takeaway

A lamp hanging beside the bed is a space saver, leaving room on your bedside table.

A bedside table is just the spot for a small display. That might be a replica of a 1960s Danish-design AJ lamp, beside a sculpture in primary colours; or a vintage radio paired with a leather camera case and silver clock; or two perfect glass bowls beside an exquisite cream-and-chrome vintage lamp.

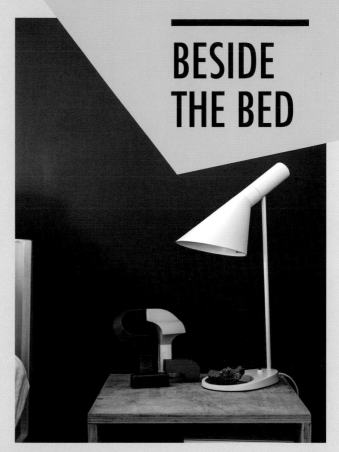

BESIDE
THE BED

One bedside option is a hanging lamp and a bedside lamp, offering two sources of light.

Jason's Takeaway

If you prefer more of a statement, opt for a larger-scale table lamp, such as the striking metal shade below.

Dark walls provide a foil for this bedroom's blend of old and new. The stripped-back chest of drawers, '60s pottery lamp, gilt-edged painting and modern three-dimensional sculpture create a distinctly personal space. The wonderful neon Graceland sign was commissioned by one of the owners for his partner, Gracie.

Jason's Takeaway

Express yourself, be original and find your own style.

A rather grand vintage chair in white and a richly coloured textured bedspread bring individuality to this bedroom.

The customised and hand-painted log-cum-bedside table has a tribal look and so does the patterned floor rug, layered on a plain rug. The linen bedding in natural shades of khaki, beige and cream blends with the room's earthy colours.

Jason's Takeaway

All the natural materials and colours echo the leafy natural view.

The wall of art in this bedroom is a collection of thrift-shop, garage sale and vintage finds, matched with layers of florals and old-fashioned tartans and comfy cushions. It's very much in keeping with the atmosphere of this weekend-in-the-country cottage.

Jason's Takeaway

This is one owner who has seriously embraced her inner collector to give her cottage its own retro style.

This looks like a magical room for a child, almost like a treehouse with its timber panelling, bare windows and greenery (inside and out!). Bright, folk art embroidery flowers on the bedcover and a jumble of cushions and handmade toys tap into the family's love of all things '70s.

The couple who live in this house have a very '70s flower-child style, and so does their home. The bedroom, with its low platform bed and mattress, has a slightly hippy look – in an upmarket sort of way – and there are pompoms on the bedding, lovely old textiles piled on the bed and rugs on top of rugs.

Jason's Takeaway

Layering adds colour and texture and warmth. Try it with throws on your sofa and bed, and with rugs overlapping on the floor.

The architecture of this early 1900s house provides a classic canvas for a marriage of old and new with the French Empire chair and modern timber bench. The colour palette is soft and the chair and wardrobe have been painted white.

Jason's Takeaway

Painting furniture a similar colour to the walls helps create an appearance of space. It also makes for a cohesive look between pieces from different periods.

A woven string macramé light fitting brings one small flourish of laidback hippy style to a fresh, all-white room.

Ceramics, an unusually shaped mirror, books and a small piece of pottery are arranged for a small but satisfying display on a shelf above the bed.

Jason's Takeaway

A shelf at eye level is a great spot to arrange favourite pieces and mementoes.

A traditional Bentwood chair gets a new twist when it's painted brilliant yellow.

Jason's Takeaway

If you are unsure how to use colour, start small, with one piece of furniture or a small area in your house.

Shelves cleverly tucked under the bed make this a wonderful reading nook.

Jason's Takeaway

This tight space is a reminder that you often have to work with what you have – this room is an example of a perfect solution.

CHANEL AND HER WORLD

Raw timber packing cases for bed bases are a no-nonsense, cost-effective solution to furnishing a bedroom. The eye-catching kids' artwork on the wall is pinned for maximum effect.

Jason's Takeaway

It's not all about how much money you spend. Innovative ideas, and a spot of DIY, can make for a stylish fit-out.

BATHROOM

THE BATHROOM – ADDING MODERN RETRO TOUCHES

Modern bathrooms can be streamlined and slick if sometimes a little boring. Introducing retro elements to the best of contemporary design and plumbing can make for an inviting space with a distinct personality. Like bedrooms, they're a place where you can be creative and invent your own retreat.

Sometimes you have to work with what you have, but don't forget to add some character or individuality. In the bathroom opposite, for example, the graphic floor tiles and monochromatic colour scheme pick up on this apartment's art deco heritage, but it's the awesome shower curtain that transforms the space. Have some fun!

You can use vintage-style tapware or an older basin to change up the look. Freestanding baths are having a resurgence, but the streamlined modern versions tap into the restrained good looks of mid-century style. Consider one of the smaller freestanding baths if space is tight.

If a complete bathroom re-do is out of the question, think about adding a vintage or retro-style stool, a stylish mirror and, my favourite, some luxurious top-quality towels to update any bathroom, retro or otherwise.

Dark penny royal tiling on the floor and up to the dado forms a strong background for the streamlined white bath and basin. The hot pink stool is all the colour that's needed.

Jason's Takeaway

If you don't have room for a chair in the bathroom, a stool is a practical addition.

Jason's Takeaway

If there's one room that needs a mirror it's a bathroom. This blonde wood mirror on a leather strap imparts a cool Nordic cabin look, but the options for different mirror styles are almost endless.

The freestanding bath has come back with a vengeance but this shapely version has an up-to-date profile. The fabulous Missoni striped bath towels inject fun, colour, pattern and interest.

With its timber lining painted green–grey, an old-fashioned basin with exposed hob tapware and a natural timber rail and stool, this bathroom could be in the country or down the coast and it could be from almost any era.

A bucket sink with navy blue trim has an edgy, industrial chic look – utilitarian but still smart. Here, it is matched with old-fashioned cross-bar tap handles.

Jason's Takeaway

Tapware can set the tone for a whole room. Search out modern versions of retro styles if that's the look you're after.

A steamy bathroom is an ideal place to tap into the trend for more indoor greenery. Consider hanging plants if surface space is limited.

Jason's Takeaway

Choose plants that enjoy a slightly tropical atmosphere, such as bamboo, ferns, spider plants and philodendron.

The original basin in a mustard colour, or harvest gold as it was sometimes known, is a vintage flashback.

Jason's Takeaway

Pairing the mustard with white tiles plays down the colour, but you could go all out and add more mustard or patterned tiles for a kitsch '70s vibe.

This marble bathroom – actually just a corner in a studio apartment – has something of a decadent '80s style. The idea of a freestanding bath is traditional but this deep black version with its minimal black tapware appears ultra modern.

A marriage of old and new, chic and industrial define this bathroom. The way the pipes have been left exposed and the handles covered in customised stitched leather sheaths turns something functional into an art piece.

Jason's Takeaway

Be original. Think about how to use retro and modern elements to make your own style.

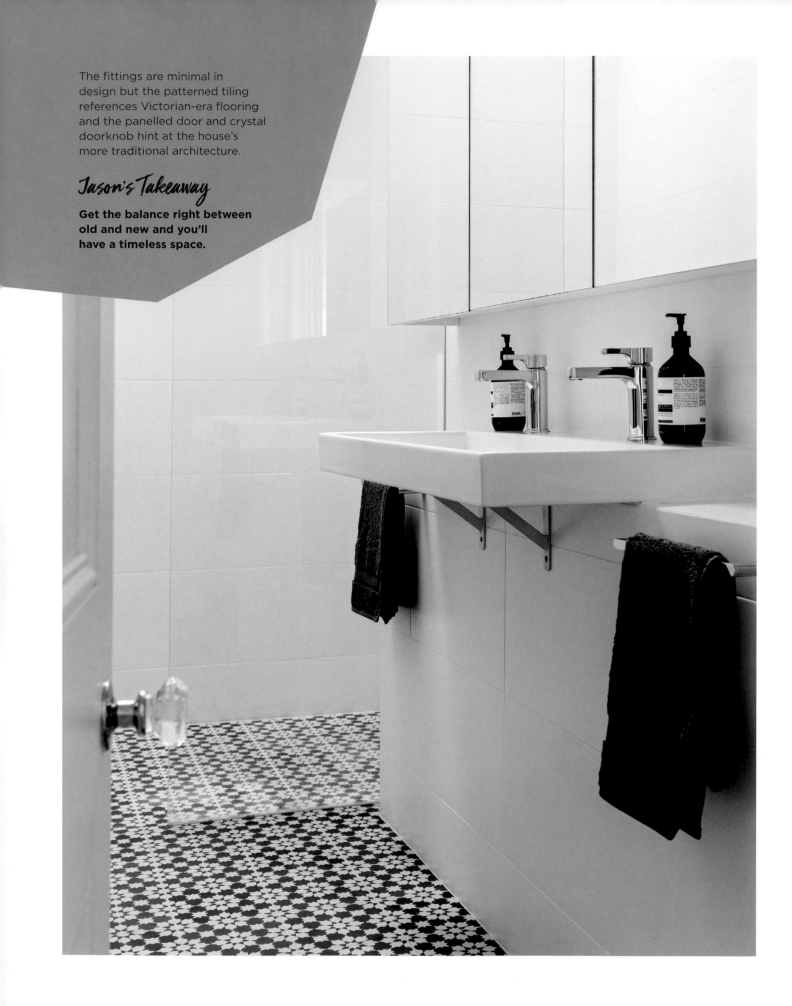

The fittings are minimal in design but the patterned tiling references Victorian-era flooring and the panelled door and crystal doorknob hint at the house's more traditional architecture.

Jason's Takeaway

Get the balance right between old and new and you'll have a timeless space.

The recess above the basin is small but fits in three storage cupboards with neat round pull handles, a shelf, wall mirror and extendable pull-out mirror. It's petite but well planned. The freestanding basin makes the bathroom seem more spacious.

Jason's Takeaway

Use good design and visual tricks to get the most out of a space.

STYLING TIPS

STYLING TIPS – CREATE YOUR PERFECT SPACE

Decorating your home is personal and should reflect who you are, your personality and how you like to live. I'm a fan of relaxed, laid-back, comfortable homes – nothing too perfect. I like things to be lived in and, of course, a little eclectic.

My own home is filled with a mix of new, vintage, designer, inexpensive and found objects. It's a little bit of everything, and it's evolved over time. I think that's a great way to decorate. Take some time, find your own way and make a space that feels like your home.

These days we're able to draw on an amazing range of design furniture and furnishings, from classic to modernist mid-century, as well as cool styles from the '70s and contemporary designs. The style of retro furnishings (which were often way ahead of their time) and designs inspired by those eras work well in 21st century interiors.

While the way you mix and match pieces will be unique, here are some basic styling guidelines, tips and tricks to help you find your own style and create your own perfect space.

COLOUR

Colour is one of the most important elements in styling your home. It has the power to establish a mood, to create an illusion of light and space or to make a room seem warm and cosy. A strong, bold colour can focus the eye, or work as a backdrop for artwork and furniture. It can be a neutral that you are not really aware of or a colour that really leaps out. White and pale shades are often thought of as neutrals, but dark colours can be neutrals too.

Many of the colours used by mid-century designers were bright. In the late '40s and '50s the primary colours of red, blue and yellow, as well as orange, citrus yellows and greens, aqua and teal became popular. And, of course, not to forget flamingo pink! In the 1960s and '70s, more earthy and autumnal shades were in vogue, with browns, russets, gold, mustard and various green shades commonly used – sometimes all of them together. Classic black and tan featured with gleaming silver chrome in stylish leather chairs, and paler creams and beige – so well suited to Danish modern furniture – made their appearance, often with white as a backdrop.

Many paint companies have retro shades from the mid-century in their colour ranges if you are seeking an authentic period look.

Using colour

▶ Not everyone can be brave with colour – it can take time. If you're not sure, start small by introducing strong colour in one or two elements.

▶ Live with a colour before you commit. See how it feels to have it in your space – paint a small section and see what you think.

▶ Use colour for a feature wall. An all-white room could have one bright yellow, orange or black wall.

▶ Use colour to zone an area, especially in a large space.

▶ If a room seems too bland, add a dash of colour (either on the walls, or with a piece of furniture, artwork or a rug) to lift it.

▶ If there's a large area of colour that is too vibrant, tone it down with some more muted colour. Or try introducing accents of other colours to break it up.

▶ If using one colour in a room, use multiple shades of it to give depth.

▶ Know your warm and cool colours. Warm colours are in the red, orange, yellow spectrum while cool colours are on the blue, green side of the colour chart. A warm grey will have some red in it, a cool grey will have blue in it. Study colour charts to see the difference.

▶ Warm colours tend to be welcoming and especially good in social areas such as dining rooms and kitchens. Cool colours are more soothing and can be effective for bedrooms or a separate study.

▶ Not all whites are equal. There are warm and cool shades, so check before painting a room icy white (unless that's what you're after).

▶ Colours are affected by other colours around them and by the light, both natural and artificial. Look at room colours at different times of day before making a final decision.

▶ Timber furniture and floors, rugs and floor coverings introduce other colours, so take these into account in the overall picture.

▶ Create a 'mood board' with swatches of the different colours, fabrics and materials that you are planning to use together.

SHAPES

Shapes play a role in how we perceive a room and even how welcoming that room can be.

Generally, our home and other constructed spaces have lots of straight lines, corners and sharp angles, which can be jarring to the eye. A simple trick to break up hard lines is to include more organic shapes in your interior.

Mid-century modern stylists were often masterful at creating this balance. While the modernist architecture might be streamlined and grid-like, furniture and light fittings introduced a whole range of striking, organic shapes: egg-shaped chairs, moulded fibreglass chairs on curved timber rockers, kidney-shaped coffee tables and fabulous, sputnik-like light pendants and furniture with multiple angles. As with texture and pattern, varying and balancing shapes adds an extra dimension to your rooms.

Using shapes

▶ A circle is one simple shape to introduce to a room to get away from the 'squareness'. This could be a circular rug, round cushions or a round table.

▶ Consider a sculptural piece of furniture, either vintage or a modern replica, to break up the grid-like pattern of a room.

▶ Light fittings – pendant lights, table lamps and floor lamps – are other options and there are myriad shapes available, in both vintage and contemporary design interpretations.

▶ Cactus and fig trees, with their giant leaves, were often used in modernist interiors to contrast with the furniture. If you prefer a softer effect, try trailing ivy or leafy ferns.

▶ Shapes within patterns, such as on wallpaper or rugs, are another way of including shapes to change the dynamics in a room. You might opt for a strong geometric pattern or a tribal design.

PATTERNS AND TEXTURES

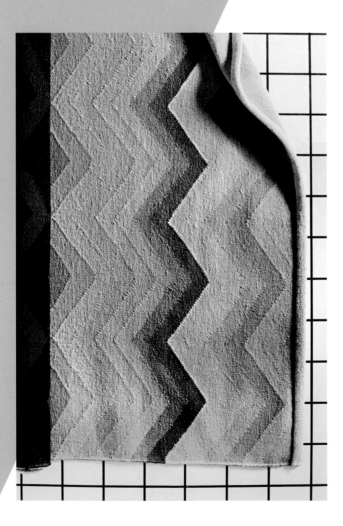

As well as using colour, pattern and texture add depth and layering to a room.

Patterns for mid-century modern textiles and furnishing fabrics were typically graphic – bold zigzags, chevrons, stripes, dots, dashes, circles and floating organic shapes were among the myriad patterns. Tropical and tribal patterns, sometimes stylised, were also in vogue.

Boldly patterned wallpapers emerged as a favourite, especially in new kitchens in the '60s and '70s. Many of the original patterns from the 20th century are now being reproduced, so have a look around for retro wallpapers.

One of the iconic names of mid-century design, famed for their patterns, is Marimekko, founded in Helsinki in the 1950s. The company's bold, often-exuberant designs appeared on fashion fabrics, furnishings and homewares. They continue to produce new designs as well as classic patterns. Include some of these fabulous fabrics for an instant hit of the '60s and '70s.

Texture is another key element to consider in any interior, and can also reference a particular era. Texture is about the surface of things, how they feel, how they catch the light and add depth to colour. For example, a mid-century modernist room from the '50s might feature polished timber, nubbly wool upholstery and soft leathers. A 1960s room could have shiny chrome for the lamps, a fluffy flokati rug and rattan and metal chairs. Move on to the '70s and you might see woven wool textiles on the wall, paper lamp shades, embroidered cushions and macramé bedcovers.

Timber, stone, metal and fabrics all add their unique textural characteristics to your home, and they usually add colour. If you are working with one colour, such as white, you can add texture within that colour family.

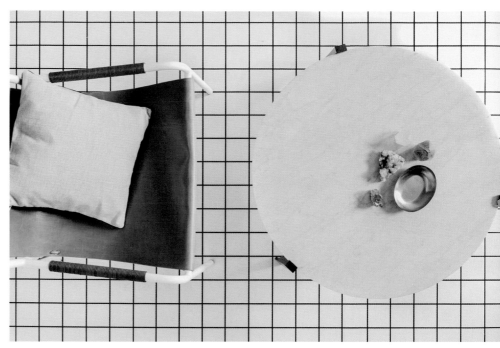

Using pattern

▶ Adding bold patterned wallpapers to a kitchen or other room will introduce a cool retro vibe, although you don't have to cover every wall to get the effect. A feature wall or splashback might be enough.

▶ Including patterns on cushion covers, curtains or upholstery for chairs or stools is another simple way to introduce a retro element.

▶ You can use different patterns together, but look for a common link (such as colour) to tie them together.

▶ Remember pattern can be subtle and still add interest.

▶ If using really bold patterns, consider toning them in with the room's colour scheme to create a modern retro look rather than a time capsule.

▶ If in doubt, start small. (Perhaps use a bold pattern, but just use a little of it.)

▶ If you prefer clashing patterns and colours, remember: rules were made to be broken!

Using texture

▶ Depending on the style you are after, cushions could be covered in velvet, linen, embroidered fabric, knits or suede to bring in some texture.

▶ When it comes to floor coverings, consider an animal hide on the floor for a sleek look, shagpile or a flokati rug for an Austin Powers–style '60s feeling, or a raffia mat for a '70s fit-out. Or you might just have smooth polished timber.

▶ A throw on your sofa can add a texture and be changed with the seasons. In winter a soft mohair rug or a Scandi-style fur will add cosiness and warmth, while in summer a cotton-knit rug or light linen throw will lighten the look.

▶ If it's more of an industrial retro look you're after, rough or timeworn timbers and exposed brick surfaces add serious texture.

▶ Decorative objects such as chunky ceramics can introduce texture to a space.

▶ Keep it balanced. If it's a modernist look you are after, you need to be a little restrained. If the '70s has more appeal, you can let your head go, with more natural textures, adding embroidery and macramé.

▶ Even the bathroom can have texture – think a mix of glossy and matt tiling (as opposed to only one finish), soft greenery and fluffy towels.

FOCAL
POINTS

Every room needs a focal point or, as I like to call it, a star of the show – a piece that catches your eye straight away. Perhaps it's a hero armchair or a spectacular pendant light or a prized artwork or feature rug. It's a piece that adds personality and something of a wow factor. Avoid too many statement pieces, though, or they will be competing with each other and you will lose the effect.

As well as individual pieces, you can create a focus with a vignette. Vignette is just a smart name for a group of *objets d'art*, a special collection or even some random found objects arranged for maximum effect. Stylists love these because they are a great way to tell a story, to bring attention to a corner, or just to look beautiful. And if you collect vintage pieces, they are also a way to introduce a retro vibe.

If you have '60s ceramics, fine glassware or mid-century pottery scattered around, gather them up and put them in a group. Arrange them on some stacked books or a tray, add a lamp, a small sculpture, a seashell … the options are endless. Think about colours and shapes and add and subtract until you are happy with the final result. Be sure to edit, though. Don't put everything on display at once. Clutter is not stylish.

SCALE AND PROPORTION

When working on any project, scale and proportion play a fundamental role in the overall design. They affect how things work together, how furniture fits a room or space and if the overall effect is harmonious. Basically, scale is the size of things and proportion is how they relate to each other.

A common mistake is to have a floor rug too small for the space and in comparison to the furniture. Take the time to measure things and consider how they fill the space. With practice you will start to see how things fit together and learn to trust your instincts.

Working with space and proportion

▶ When furnishing a living space, the sofa is usually the key piece, so start with that and add other pieces that 'relate' to it in size. For example, if the sofa is large you need a coffee table that works proportionately.

▶ Always measure pieces before you buy them to make sure they fit in your room (and through the door) and then measure how much space they will occupy in the room. Measure twice and buy once!

▶ If a rug is to go under a sofa or dining table, make sure it extends beyond the furniture so that it looks comfortable, not cramped.

▶ A small room doesn't mean you have to have a lot of dolls' house–size furniture. Sometimes a couple of large pieces look more generous.

▶ If hanging artwork over a fireplace or sideboard, take into account the size of the painting relative to what's below it. A little painting hanging in the middle of a wide space will look wrong because the proportions don't relate.

▶ If you have space, think about adding some oversize pieces – a large artwork, a substantial pendant lamp or giant pot plant – for some drama or special focus.

▶ Not everything has to be the same scale, but things do need to relate to each other. Is the coffee table the right height for the sofa? Is the bedside table high enough or do you have to reach down?

▶ Consider the flow in a room – can you walk around the sofa, pull out the chair from a table, reach the television without falling over something. It's all about the space and proportion of pieces that fill this space.

LIGHTING

Good lighting makes all the difference to your home. It sets a tone and creates a mood, and with interesting light fittings, it's a chance to add personality. Lighting also needs to serve practical requirements. I'm a fan of multiple light sources in a room, so that you can adjust the light to suit different tasks, focus on different spaces within a room, and generally create ambience.

Retro lights

Mid-century modern designers came up with some incredible designs and many styles have stayed in production or are now made again.

There are several key types of light in particular where you can channel a retro vibe in a modern interior – pendant lamps, floor lamps, table and desk lamps. The array of styles to choose from – original vintage, contemporary replicas and designs inspired by previous eras – is impressive.

Pendants

Not only functional but potentially highly decorative, pendants are your chance to make a design statement. Pendants are perfect in hallways as they create a point of interest in a sometimes difficult space. They work well in living areas, particularly when there are also floor or table lamps. They are perfectly suited for rooms with high ceilings, but can be adjusted for lower ceilings as well (you need to think about the scale and proportion). Over a table, a pendant creates a focus on the dining area. Pendants also work over a bench, especially when used in multiples, as they cast different areas of light. Remember – the larger the area to be lit, the bigger the pendant needed. The light will cast a wider glow.

Floor Lamps

Floor lamps can shine up or down depending on their style and are particularly good for living spaces. You can place a floor lamp in a corner or a spot where the light can bounce off the floor or wall or ceiling. They add height, and lighting a room from different heights adds dimension to it. Because of their height, floor lamps can also add to the overall visual balance of a room.

Table and desk lamps

Table and desk lamps are useful for spotlighting, task lighting, accent and ambient lighting.

They can make a bright corner in a dark room, or direct the focus. Table lamps can add style but still satisfy practical demands. Put them on side tables, bedside tables, hall tables and sideboards. Many of the mid-century modern styles were in metal or glass and look every bit as good today as they did fifty or more years ago.

A few points about using lights

▶ Use light to draw people into a room, to create a focal point and to draw attention to artwork or an architectural feature.

▶ Don't forget the practical aspect. Different rooms need different light sources and levels. A kitchen needs light bright enough for working and eating, while a bedroom needs more subdued lighting with bedside lamps for reading.

▶ For task lighting, such as on a desk or for working in the kitchen, lights that can be adjusted with a moveable arm or extension are more versatile.

▶ A lightshade doesn't have to be expensive. Low-cost Chinese paper-and-bamboo lantern shades, popular in the '70s, are making a comeback.

▶ If you do buy vintage light fittings, always check with an electrician that the wiring is safe and that they can be used with modern sockets and bulbs.

ABOUT THE AUTHOR

Mr Jason Grant is a Sydney-based interior stylist and author. He has worked with many Australian and international magazines, collaborated with exciting major brands and created a signature home collection of his own (www.mjgstore.com).

This is his third book, a follow-up to *A Place Called Home* and *Holiday at Home*.

Follow Jason on Instagram @mrjasongrant or on his blog mrjasongrant.com.

ABOUT THE PHOTOGRAPHER

Lauren Bamford is a professional photographer, based in Melbourne, Australia, who specialises in food, lifestyle, interiors and documentary photography. Lauren is regularly commissioned by international publications and advertising agencies.

Maintaining an unobtrusive approach to her subjects, Lauren has also developed a large body of personal photography work, which has been exhibited at various art galleries including the National Gallery of Victoria.

Check out more of her work at laurenbamford.com or follow her on Instagram @laurenbamford.

THANK YOU

I'm one lucky guy, living my dream (with a lot of hustle and hard work!) with the cutest dog in the world. Yes, you will spot Sophia, my Boston Terrier, throughout this book.

I can't do anything alone. I'm very lucky to have a great team of people that helps across all I do, especially when it comes to books. For those who have been involved in a big or small way – thank you. Collaboration is always the key.

A huge thanks to Lauren Bamford, the book's photographer, for her hard work and enthusiasm. It's been a big project but we did it!

Thanks to all the awesome homeowners for inviting us into their homes and sharing their spaces with us. You really are this book! Orlando and Greg, Miranda, Simone, Tom, Grazia, Katie, Lyn, Harold and Andy, Stuart and Simmo, Jason and Nathan, Dion and Grace, Hans and Ursula, Belinda, Sam, Julie, Scott and Poppie, Madeleine, Phillip, Andy and Ben – your homes are all unique and beautiful.

A special thanks to a few wonderful friends who helped work some magic – Clare Patience, The Broad Place, Mark and Barry and Natalie. And, of course, thanks to Paul, Melissa, Margaret, Anna, designers Mark and Kate and the entire Hardie Grant team. Dreams do come true.

I'm thrilled with what I do and for everyone who believes in me, thank you. Also a big thanks to you, the reader, really the most important part of this process, for enjoying my sense of style. Decorating your home should be fun! I hope you're inspired by book three, and I'd love to see my book in your space. Don't forget to share your pics on Instagram.

Published in 2017 by Hardie Grant Books,
an imprint of Hardie Grant Publishing

Hardie Grant Books (Melbourne)
Building 1, 658 Church Street
Richmond, Victoria 3121
hardiegrantbooks.com.au

Hardie Grant Books (London)
5th & 6th Floors
52–54 Southwark Street
London SE1 1UN
hardiegrantbooks.co.uk

A Cataloguing-in-Publication entry is available from
the catalogue of the National Library of Australia at
www.nla.gov.au

Modern Retro Home
ISBN 978 1 74270 992 5

Commissioning Editor: Melissa Kayser
Managing Editor: Marg Bowman
Project Editor: Anna Collett
Editor: Margaret Barca
Design Manager: Mark Campbell
Designer: Kate Barraclough
Photographer: Lauren Bamford
Production Manager: Todd Rechner
Production Coordinator: Rebecca Bryson

Colour reproduction by
Splitting Image Colour Studio
Printed in China by
1010 Printing International Limited